TOO MANY EMAILS

Managing Them Instead of Them Managing You

TONY JEARY

with
MARC HARTY
GEORGE LOWE
SARA BOWLING

TOO MANY EMAILS

By Tony Jeary
with Marc Harty, George Lowe, and Sara Bowling

CornerStone
Leadership Institute

www.**cornerstoneleadership**.com

ISBN: 0-9746403-0-1

Printed in the United States of America
10 9 8 7 6 5 4 3 2 1
Edited by ATW Training & Consulting, Inc.

Commitment to Efficiency

We're now in the 21st century and email is clearly a major part of our personal and professional lives. I believe everyone would agree there is an opportunity to enhance email effectiveness personally and throughout our organizations. We may spend as much as one or two hours a day just managing our emails. Email is really just a new form of presenting, a new way to communicate our ideas, grow our businesses, and transfer information and knowledge.

We've developed this handbook with tips to increase your email efficiency and fit most situations you will face in sending and receiving emails. You could possibly save 30 minutes – or more – a day, if you will commit to adopting many of the ideas contained within this handbook. Read and choose the tips and techniques that will make a difference for you.

Sincerely,

Tony

Tony Jeary – Mr. Presentation™

Table of Contents

HOW EFFICIENT IS YOUR EMAIL? 7

PHILOSOPHY 8

   What is an e-presentation? 10
   What you'll get from reading this book 11

INCOMING EMAIL 12

OUTGOING EMAIL 20

   Be brief 22
   Be clear 24
   Be simple 26
   Be prompt 27
   Be careful 28
   Other outgoing email tips 30

SAVING TIME AND CREATING TEAM CULTURE 36

GLOBAL TIPS 40

APPENDIX 46

   List of abbreviations 47
   Standards checklist 48

HOW EFFICIENT IS YOUR EMAIL?

**If you check any of the following,
this handbook is for you.**

❏ Is email an important part of your daily life?

❏ Do you get over 50 emails a day and often can't make time to read them all?

❏ Would you like to save hours every week by becoming more effective and efficient with email?

❏ Do you regularly receive emails that are too long and unclear?

❏ Do you tire of having too many carbon copy and blind carbon copy emails in your inbox?

❏ Would you like to have the people who send you emails understand better how you'd like to receive them?

PHILOSOPHY

"Technology is a weird thing; it brings you great gifts with one hand, and it stabs you in the back with the other."

C.P. Snow

What is an e-presentation?

An e-presentation is simply a presentation made electronically. E-presentations are made by PowerPoint, on the internet, in DVD and CD formats, and of course the most popular of all—email. In today's electronic culture, e-presentation skills and etiquette should be studied, learned, and practiced. **Too Many Emails** is about email presentation mastery. Such a skill wasn't needed a few years ago, but it is absolutely essential today.

Many people have good writing skills, effective communication abilities, and technical know-how, but few apply these talents successfully with email. **Too Many Emails** will show you how to master email.

What you'll get from reading this book

Email differs from other methods of communication because it is instantaneous, impersonal, and usually irreversible. Additionally, this widely-used communication tool enables the same message to be simultaneously sent to a broad distribution group.

Through email you and your colleagues can now manage meetings, action items, strategic plans, and almost every other aspect of business. Many have learned their email skills by default rather than via specific training. As a result, **unless email is properly utilized, time and money can be wasted with every email sent and received.**

We've all received emails that were poorly constructed, inefficiently distributed, or contained inappropriate content. Maybe we've even been guilty of sending such communications.

Too Many Emails will give you the tools and techniques to create a culture of email effectiveness. As you read this handbook, highlight tips, strategies, and skills you can apply to email. Record your comments as you concentrate on one section at a time. You can learn to manage email effectively and efficiently. These best practices and examples are practical steps to make email easy.

Note: There are exceptions to virtually any of the guidelines and rules suggested within **Too Many Emails**. Each person and organization has their own circumstances, styles, and systems. So, as you read and study each of these suggestions, filter what works for you, and highlight the ideas you need to implement.

Section One
INCOMING EMAIL

Face-to-face communication breaks down to approximately 55% body language, 38% tone of voice, and 7% content.

Be cognizant that when you communicate with email, you eliminate 55% of usual communication.

Being organized and streamlined is important when handling incoming email. You can achieve email efficiency by keeping a clean in-box, creating and using filters and folders, and deleting and archiving emails frequently.

1 Keep A Clean In-Box

Use your in-box as a landing strip for incoming email. As you receive new messages, they should be immediately dealt with appropriately and then filed or deleted.

2 One-Touch Rule

Remember the one-touch rule: when you receive a new message, "touch" it once (take action, file or delete).

3 Sort Incoming Mail

Use a method for sorting incoming mail. Explore your email application's capabilities to be more efficient.

4 Prioritize and Discard Incoming Mail

Junk mail can automatically be sent to the trash bin. Mail from designated individuals or sent to specific groups can be flagged and filed. Action items can be prioritized.

5 "To Review" Folder

Non-urgent emails can be stored in a "To Review" folder for later review.

6 Descriptive Folders

Manually move messages into descriptive folders with titles such as Action Required, Save, Pending, Personal, Month, Project, Name, etc.

7 Save with Dates

When saving incoming mail, use a date system for organizing the emails as well as the attachments. You will be more efficient when you create a logical storage and retrieval system.

8 Delete And Archive Frequently

Don't hesitate to use the delete key, especially if you receive large volumes of email. Also, don't feel pressed to read every email; delete what you can as soon as it enters your in-box.

9 Why You Should Delete

The fewer unnecessary emails you save and the more organized your folders, the easier it will be to perform searches, both manually and via your email application. Eliminate clutter and your email application may run more efficiently when downloading messages or opening attachments.

10 Not Important, Delete

If the email doesn't have important information to you or to your organization, delete it immediately.

11 When Complete, Delete

Delete emails that relate to actions you've performed or obligations you've fulfilled when no other pertinent important information is contained in the message.

12 If it's a Repeat, Delete

Delete email reply components, especially if the entire original is included in the latest version.

13 FYI Only, Delete

Review and delete emails designated "FYI" only.

14 Mailing-List Email, Delete

Delete mailing list emails if you have no intention of reading them soon (and consider removing your name from the mailing list altogether if you find the content is not valuable to you and your goals).

15 Old and Cold, Delete

Some emails you need to keep for a while, but when you find those are old and no longer necessary, delete.

16 Attachments Saved, Delete

Delete email with large attachments that you've saved elsewhere on your computer. Attachments take up valuable space—and lots of it.

17 *Archive Often*

An archive is on-line storage that takes specific emails and saves them in a condensed format on your hard drive or disk. This saves valuable space and allows you to keep old items you may refer to in the future. For ease in sorting, use specific folders for archived email.

If you're still apprehensive to delete items, archiving is a safe alternative.

18 *Forward Regularly*

Often emails come to you that simply need skimmed or not read at all, just forwarded to an assistant, associate, co-worker, etc. Save yourself time by being keenly aware of what can and should be forwarded.

19 *Print and Go*

You can print emails, put them in a file and carry with you to read, study, and take notes during a commute, flight, or other slow times (waiting in lines, waiting in a doctor's office, etc.)

20 *Saving is an Art*

Sometimes (especially in lengthy emails), it is better to save the email, if needed, in the right file rather than read it. Then you can refer to it if the need arises.

21 *Assistant Sort*

Many busy managers and executives fail to delegate email responsibilities to competent employees. If applicable, ask yourself, should someone else be sorting, organizing, forwarding, and even answering at least part (if not the majority) of your incoming emails.

> *"When something can be read without effort, great effort has gone into its writing."*

Enrique Jardiel Poncela

Section Two
OUTGOING EMAIL

The five "Bs" of email presentations

1. Be brief
2. Be clear
3. Be simple
4. Be prompt
5. Be careful

Be brief

Most of us were educated to write entire paragraphs comprised of complete sentences. While this method is appropriate in many situations, it is not always best when composing emails. Phrases, bullets, and acceptable abbreviations shave time off both the construction of messages as well as reading received messages.

A Lengthy Example

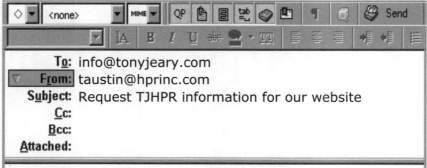

To: info@tonyjeary.com
From: taustin@hprinc.com
Subject: Request TJHPR information for our website
Cc:
Bcc:
Attached:

Hi Wendy,

First, regarding our request to add TJHPR information to our website, have you had an opportunity to talk with Chris, our website manager? Second, I just wanted to see if I could provide you with additional information or answer any questions you may have about what we are requesting. Please let me know what I can do to assist you in moving this request forward.

Thank you.

Kevin

A Brief Alternative

Wendy,

Have you spoken with Chris, our website manager, about adding TJHPR information to our website?

Do you require any more information or have any questions?

Kevin

22 Value Time

Many recipients will not have the time or interest to review lengthy, complicated messages - email should be concise and to the point. Are your emails brief, clear and simple?

23 Brief is Best

When requesting a specific outcome or relaying information, brief is best. Sometimes, brief needs only to fill in the subject line (refer to Subject line Message below).

24 Subject Line Message

Use the subject line as the entire message, inserting "EOM" for "end of message" at the conclusion. For example,
Subject: Manger meeting cancelled today – EOM

25 Rule of Thumb...1 Screen

Attempt to keep emails to one screen length or shorter.

26 Keep Paragraphs Short

Keep your paragraphs to 4-5 lines each. Others will find your message easier to read in short paragraph form.

Be clear

Being clear in your messages is just as essential as being brief.

27 State the Topic in Subject Line

Specifically state the topic in the subject line. Using a detailed subject line helps the recipient easily identify your message and locate it quickly from an archive folder. Perhaps state the topic followed by a colon and more details (i.e., Nov. Staff Meeting: Proposed Agenda).

28 Use Qualifiers in the Subject Line

In the subject line, use "FYI" for "for your information" and use "urgent" or "action required" when you desire a quick response. Do not overuse "Urgent" or it will lose its impact. For example,

Subject: Urgent: customer response re: order shipment
Subject: FYI: out-of-town August 4-8

29 Think Through Questions and Requests

Be clear with questions and/or requests. Eliminate response emails requesting clarification by thinking through all aspects of the topic and addressing them in your initial email.

30 Assume Little

Don't assume the recipient knows what you need or want. Explain yourself thoroughly (but remember to be brief).

31 Use Slang or Jargon Carefully

Avoid using slang or jargon that is not clearly understood. The receiver may not be familiar with your language or terminology, but even if they are, less is more. Cutting a few words and phrases from each email can save time.

32 Spell Check

Always before sending, perform a spell check, especially for business emails going to prospects and customers. Spell check takes only seconds and can ensure your credibility is maintained as well as the clarity of your message is intact. Some programs can even be set to auto spell check after you hit the 'send' button.

33 Spam Check

Many people are installing spam filters to intercept emails before they reach the in-box. Certain email characteristics may lump your email with unsolicited messages. To ensure your message is delivered, avoid writing your subject line in all capital letters or using words like "free" and "offer."

> ## *"Verbosity leads to unclear, inarticulate things."*
>
> *Dan Quayle*

Be simple

34 *Use Bullets, Numbered Lists & Separators*

Use bulleted phrases, numbered lists, and separated paragraphs (instead of tabs) to make your message visually easier to read.

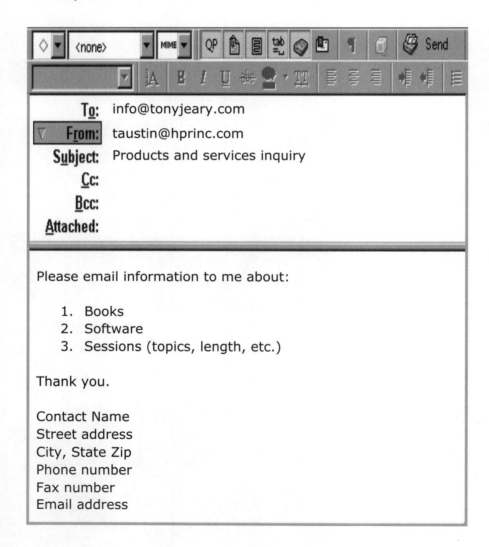

To: info@tonyjeary.com
From: taustin@hprinc.com
Subject: Products and services inquiry
Cc:
Bcc:
Attached:

Please email information to me about:

1. Books
2. Software
3. Sessions (topics, length, etc.)

Thank you.

Contact Name
Street address
City, State Zip
Phone number
Fax number
Email address

Be Prompt

When possible, respond immediately to an email. Responding promptly will fulfill the sender's request and complete a task off your to-do list.

35 *Same Business Day Response*

Respond to work email within the same business day, and respond to personal email within one to three business days as a general rule.

36 *Inform Sender of Status*

If you cannot immediately complete a requested task or supply necessary information, send a short email informing the sender of your intention to reply.

37 *Meet Deadlines*

If you set a deadline to follow-up or complete a task, meet the deadline. Honoring your word and being dependable builds you a solid reputation.

38 *Be Consistent*

Be consistent with your responses so recipients know what to expect from you.

Be careful

Unlike paper letters that can be removed from the mailbox before the post arrives or later shredded, email is virtually permanent, irreversible, and can be shared with others. Furthermore, deleted messages can later be resurrected. Use discretion and caution when sending messages containing personal information because a confidential email message does not exist.

39 *If You Wouldn't Want it in Print, Don't Write It*

Don't write anything in an email you would not want in the newspaper or addressed in a court of law.

40 *Misinterpretations are Common*

Misinterpretations can easily occur when using email. Pay attention to your tone, use humor carefully, and avoid sarcasm completely.

41 *Keep it Clean*

Don't send gossip or nasty emails. Be discreet and send only appropriate business information. Even though the temptation may be great, or the recipient may seem trustworthy, keep in mind emails can be forwarded (accidentally or purposely), printed, and even read aloud.

42 Anger Danger

Don't send an email written in a fit of anger. Consider writing down your thoughts and using the telephone instead. Count to 10 (or 100!) before making the call. Or, write the response and wait a day, reread it again, adjust as needed, and then send.

43 Consider Alternatives

Email may be swift and simple to use, but cannot completely replace handwritten notes, phone calls, or face-to-face meetings. Consider the best communication method when you need to convey thanks, criticism, praise, or complaints.

44 When In Doubt, Don't Send It Out!

If you are questioning whether or not to send an email for any reason, don't send it. If it's important, clarity will come and you can send it then. Otherwise, you will undoubtedly save yourself a lot of grief by abstaining.

> *"Man does not live by words alone, but he sometimes has to eat them."*
>
> *Adlai Stevenson*

Other Outgoing Email Tips

45 *Identify Yourself Every Time*

Emails can all look alike; it's imperative for the recipient to know the sender's identity. Furthermore, the recipient may need other ways to contact you besides email. One way to accomplish this is to create a standard signature that includes pertinent information. Here's an example of information to include in your signature:

46 International Codes

If you conduct business in a different country, be sure to include international codes with your phone number; not all of your recipients will always know how to reach you from other countries.

47 Tagline Cautions

Include a tagline or motto, but care should be taken when using certain quotations or references, or anything else that might be misinterpreted or cause offense. It's best to keep taglines business focused or don't use one.

48 Using Style/Formatting

Formatting can go a long way to enhance your message, provide clarity or emphasis, and even give some personality to your emails. However, don't overburden your recipients with fancy stationery or backgrounds, strange fonts, odd colors, blinking text, or large graphics. If you really want to incorporate a human touch, send your letter on paper instead.

49 Are You Compatible?

Due to incompatibility between email applications, some information may not appear in your message or will appear as gibberish, depending on the recipient's applicaiton. Whenever possible, use plain text rather than html since plain text is almost universally understood by most email applications.

Email Graphic Alternatives to Consider

Utilize the following tips unless you are certain the recipient uses the same email application you do and will be able to see formatting and color.

50 *Italics Alternative*

Use _book title_ instead of italicizing. For example, "I just finished reading _A Purpose Driven Life_."

51 *Dashes Instead of Bullets*

For greatest compatibility, use dashes instead of automatic bullets. Number lists manually.

52 *Symbols Instead of Color*

Instead of highlighting with color, designate comments with symbols preceding each comment.

53 *Asterisks or CAPS for Emphasis*

Use asterisks (*) to provide clarity and add emphasis to words or phrases. Emphasis can also be conveyed by using all caps, but do not overuse. Remember, when you use capital letters, it can be interpreted as you are shouting.

54 Don't Waste Bandwidth

Not only is time precious in today's business world, space is an issue. When sending emails, keep in mind messages take up actual space on a server somewhere. If you are careful with bandwidth utilization, your server will be uncluttered and therefore not overburdened.

55 Carbon Copy

Use care when adding names to the 'cc' (carbon copy) field. Really consider if all recipients need to receive the email you're sending. Value their time. Save time by using 'cc' to include people who need to know the information contained in an email.

56 Replying to All

If you receive an email with a large 'cc' list, don't "Reply to All" unless absolutely necessary. It's best to hand-pick the appropriate individuals and send a reply only to them. Again, consider saving the time of others.

57 Blind Carbon Copy

When sending an email to a large number of people, use the 'bcc' (blind carbon copy) field for addresses. Send the message to yourself in the 'to' field. This will prevent mass subsequent mailing to the entire list, and ensure privacy is maintained.

58 Blind Carbon Copy Reply

Don't "Reply to All" when you've been sent an email as a 'bcc' recipient. The sender might not want others on the recipient list to know you've been blind carbon copied.

59 Compress Large Attachments

Don't send large attachments; compress anything larger than 300 kb if possible. Various compression software applications are available. Research and obtain one that works for you (Winzip and Stuffit are two of the most common).

60 Compress Multiple Attachments

Compressing can also be useful when sending multiple files, regardless of individual size.

61 Rename Revised Documents

If you alter or revise an attachment and then re-send, rename the document to show a more current version date and/or number (even re-date the subject line).

62 Strings and Threads

When forwarding or replying to an email that contains a "string" or "thread" (a chain of emails all relating to one another), make sure the recipient(s) can decipher who wrote what comments. When possible, only send the pertinent information and delete the rest.

63 Don't Send Junk Mail

For professional communication, avoid sending forwarded jokes, chain letters, non-work related messages, etc. (and ask that others stop sending junk mail to you). Many organizations have policies against sending non-work related emails.

64 Archiving And Deleting

If you often delete your sent emails, consider turning off the "save sent items" option. Instead, carbon copy (cc) or blind carbon copy (bcc) yourself only on messages you really need to save. Retain messages that required a lot of effort to create, relate to customers, or are very detailed.

65 Don't Call it Urgent if It's Not

Refrain from marking every email as "high priority" or "urgent." Over time, it may become the classic "boy who cried wolf" story; no one will believe it's urgent.

66 Virus Threats

Use extreme caution when forwarding messages related to computer virus threats. Hoaxes can be researched and verified through various web sites. Consider the following before forwarding a threat:

- Did a trained computer security expert send you the alert?
- Does it urge you to forward the email to everyone you know? If so, it is probably a hoax.
- Does the email offer a link to an authoritative details page?

"The small words work best and the old small words work best of all."

Winston Churchill

Section Three
SAVING TIME
AND
CREATING TEAM
CULTURE

> *"The problem with communication is the illusion that it has occurred."*
>
> *George Bernard Shaw*

*I*mplementing the ideas contained in this book will reduce wasted time and increase productivity. However, these positive results will not reach maximum effectiveness if only a few individuals within your organization choose to change their email habits. Others in your group or company will be more apt to incorporate your tips if you demonstrate the ease of use and amount of time saved—benefits to them.

Changing an organization's culture is not easy. Habits and processes are major components of an organization's culture. Bad habits hurt; good habits bring strength. Be committed to stimulating change in your culture for more efficient use of email.

The following tips are ways you can begin to gain buy-in from your colleagues:

67 *Save Frequently-Used Content*

Create an arsenal of frequently used email content. Standard emails will eliminate recreating and promote consistency.

68 *Fill in the Blanks*

When sending messages based on a template from your arsenal, don't forget to complete the missing information, such as recipient name ("Dear _____") or date, etc.

69 *Personalize Templates*

Personalize a line or two to make the template seem less impersonal.

70 *Utilize Shared Network*

Place any commonly-utilized templates in shared network folders so your entire team can benefit from the arsenal.

71 *Create an Arsenal Folder*

Create an easily-accessible folder (for personal or group use) that contains frequently-used attachments.

72 *Create a Standards Checklist*

Create a standards checklist you can use with your colleagues, direct reports, and anyone else who needs to use the techniques in this handbook. Refer to the Appendix for a sample standards checklist.

Section Four
GLOBAL TIPS

"Those who write clearly have readers; those who write obscurely have commentators."

Albert Camus

73 Use a Salutation

Use a salutation (Hi, Dear, etc.) with a first name.

74 Avoid Setting Unreasonable Deadlines

Avoid setting unreasonable deadlines when making requests. You cannot know the schedule or priorities of the recipient and an immediate response may be impossible. Also, you cannot know how often the recipient checks his or her email. Some people check email every 10 minutes, while others check once a day (or less frequently when traveling). When you need something quickly, it's really best to phone the individual instead.

75 Recognize Time Zone Differences

Pay attention to time zone differences when setting deadlines or scheduling meetings.

76 Before Sending, Double-Check

Before sending, don't just spell check. Also perform a quick assessment to ensure the recipient's address is correct. Especially in large organizations, email addresses may be quite similar and a quick check could save time and embarrassment later.

77 Close Your Email to Focus

Close your email application when you need to concentrate on a task. Don't interrupt your focus just to read or respond to email.

78 Check Emails at Predetermined Intervals

Many of us are distracted when we hear the chime announce a new email has arrived. If you need uninterrupted time to think and work, consider checking and responding to emails at regular intervals each day. For example, check your email four times a day.

79 Remote Email

Determine how you can check your email from remote sites. You will find this helpful when traveling or if your computer malfunctions.

80 Auto-responders

If you will be out of the office for longer than a day, turn on your email auto-responder. This sends an automatic reply with specific information to anyone who sends you an email. Others will appreciate knowing you are unavailable and your intentions for responding when you return. For example, "I will be on vacation from Jan. 26 through Feb. 2, and will not be checking email. If you need immediate assistance, please call Joe at 972-555-1111. I look forward to connecting with you when I return."

81 For Immediate Response, Notify Recipient

If you need an immediate response to an email, consider calling and alerting the recipient.

82 New Hires

In new employee orientation, include company policies on email.

83 *Create an Email Database*

When receiving incoming emails, create a database by saving email addresses and other relevant information received with emails.

APPENDIX

List of abbreviations

AFIK: as far as I know

ASAP: as soon as possible

BCC: blind carbon copy

BTW: by the way

CC: carbon copy

CNP: continued on next page

EOM: end of message

FYI: for your information

GMTA: great minds think alike

IMHO: in my humble opinion

IMO: in my opinion

JMHO: just my humble opinion

JMO: just my opinion

JTLYK: just to let you know

OTTOMH: off the top of my head

PM: private message

PTB: powers that be

SYS: see you soon

TBD: to be determined

TIA: thanks in advance

TTBOMK: to the best of my knowledge

WB: welcome back

Standards checklist

1. **State your topic**
   - ❑ Fill the topic line
   - ❑ Flag it with a descriptive topic
   - ❑ Write "urgent" for quick response—even use FYI to clarify why you are sending

2. **Be brief**
   - ❑ Keep emails to one screen length when possible
   - ❑ If you want a quick response, be brief in your request

3. **Style counts**
   - ❑ Use bulleted phrases
   - ❑ Use numbered lists
   - ❑ Use short, separated paragraphs

4. **Identify yourself**
   - ❑ Create a standard signature you always attach
   - ❑ Include your full name, title, phone number and other pertinent contact information
   - ❑ Include tag line or motto if applicable—remember to keep it brief

5. **Answer promptly**
   - ❑ Answer work email within the same day when possible
   - ❑ Answer personal email within three days
   - ❑ Be consistent with your responses so recipients will know what to expect
   - ❑ Use auto-responders when you will be unavailable for a day or longer

6. **Be careful what you say**
   - ❑ What you write is permanent
   - ❑ Don't respond in anger—save a draft and review later

7. **Delete frequently**
   - ❑ Keep a clean mailbox
   - ❑ Create folders to organize your emails
   - ❑ Smaller amounts of emails = less stress
   - ❑ Delete emails you don't need for future reference

8. **Manage your 'cc'**
   - ❑ Only use CC's when really needed
   - ❑ If you receive CC's, read then and file or delete immediately

9. **Say 'NO' to junk mail**
   - ❑ Don't forward chain letters—they cause stress and aggravation
   - ❑ Resist forwarding jokes and stories that are unrelated to someone you specifically know

10. **Don't forget the personal touch**
    - ❑ Don't miss out on the power of a personal handwritten note
    - ❑ When a phone call is best, make it

11. **Build an email database**
    - ❑ Save email addresses
    - ❑ Email relevant or useful items to those in your arsenal (share the wealth)

12. **Build an email etiquette culture**
    - ❑ Influence others to use time saving techniques when communicating

ACCELERATED ACHIEVEMENT STRATEGIC PLANNING

Tony Jeary has been the CEO of several multi-million-dollar companies and understands the bottom-line impact of strategic planning. In a truly unique, half-day planning session with Tony, you will accomplish results that would normally take days. Tony and the HPR team will lead you through the creation of a one-page WordZar™ Matrix for each of the following four processes for making strategic planning painless, purposeful, and extremely powerful:

1 **SWOT Overview Matrix** – Tony helps you build a solid foundation for your strategic plan through an intense exercise that identifies your organization's specific strengths, weaknesses, opportunities, and threats.

2 **Strategic Plan Matrix** – You will come away with an extremely action-oriented plan and a focused set of objectives and supporting tactics. You will also identify the people in your organization responsible for executing the plan.

3 **Branding Process Matrix** – Tony's skillful ability to hone in on key ideas will unleash the power of branding for your organization, product, process, or personality. The questions in the branding process have been crafted to help you define what you want the market to think of your brand, the core purpose of your brand, what barriers exist for your brand, and more.
The process is compounded by applying the content of the Branding Process Matrix to a critical review of an organization's current marketing collateral. The basis for this powerful exercise is Tony's simply administered 68-question audit featured in Tony's book, *Presenting Your Business Visually.*

4 **Performance Standards Matrix** – Tony has mastered the ability to lead organizations in an amazingly short amount of time to craft a set of precise standards that enables the team to operate at peak performance.

Tony Facilitates group buy-in

In a single session with Tony and his team, you will take advantage of...

- Internal Benchmarking – Tony will help you bring your organization's best ideas to the forefront.

- External Benchmarking - Because Tony coaches executives from so many different companies, he is able to cross-pollinate "best practices" from one industry to another.

- Knowledge Arsenal – Tony has created this powerful toolchest as a result of more than two decades of dedicated and voracious study. It is a rare collection of presentation, strategic planning, and business acumen that includes thousands of book summaries, manuals, samples, and research on dozens of topics that are available to all clients at no charge.

www.tonyjeary.com

Tony Jeary has a unique ability to blend strategy, team synergy, and organizational momentum.

"Get your business in TOP shape today! Call for a FREE packet of samples and examples of what Tony has done for others"

SUCCESS ACCELERATION BOOTCAMP

The Presenter's Studio™

"This day was truly one of the most powerful days of my life, on both a personal and business level."

Success is accelerated by learning and applying proven principles from successful people who have come before us. Tony Jeary has done precisely that. From more than 20 years of intense study and application, he has developed a one-day Experience, based on his book *Success Acceleration*, that is overflowing with proven and dynamic principles that will expedite your way to success.

Comprised of Four Modules, each supported by one of Tony's highly acclaimed Books.

Designing Your Own Life

The journey begins even before you arrive. Using Tony's step-by-step guide, you will develop a solid foundation for building a successful life. This special binder will be further completed during the course of the workshop as we look at all the facets of the "Balance Wheel of Life" — the values that drive you and the true goals you want to achieve.

Business Strategies for Peak Performance

Building upon your goals and values, we develop a concise plan for taking your business to the desired level. We work with you to identify operating strategies that support your vision. Each strategy will be assigned a set of specific, tactical actions for making your vision a reality (quick, simple, and efficient).

Presenting Your Business Visually

This is a 68-question audit to evaluate aspects of marketing that apply to virtually every business. From defining public relations and paid advertising to coordinating business cards, web sites, and fax coversheets, this exercise will show you how to maximize your marketing efforts, build your brand, and help you bring prospects to you.

Inspire Any Audience

Finally, you will discover how to more effectively present your spoken message. This module is based on Tony Jeary's best selling book *Inspire Any Audience*. You will learn to develop presentations in a short amount of time and deliver your message in a way that will help you sell more, work a room better, and leverage every presentation you make.

"Only four dates this year, Call NOW to register"

About the Authors

Tony Jeary – Mr. Presentation™

Tony Jeary personally teaches world-class organizations how to be more effective communicators. His company, Tony Jeary High Performance Resources, has worked for more than 500 organizations in more than thirty-five countries. Their clients include the presidents, CEOs, and entire organizations of Ford, Wal-Mart, New York Life, EDS, Cingular Wireless, IBM and many other Fortune 100 companies. Contact his business manager at dan@tonyjeary.com to discuss speaking, coaching and unique strategic planning opportunities with Tony and his team.

Marc Harty

Marc Harty is one of the leading e-communications strategists in the country. Marc bring a proven track record of helping organizations communicate more effectively and sell more convincingly via digital media. Marc is author of *Strategic Traffic: How to Generate Thousands of Targeted Web Site Visitors at Zero Advertising Cost*. Visit his website at www.StrategicTraffic.com. He speaks regularly on email communications, search engine marketing and web traffic conversion.

George Lowe

George Lowe established his consulting practice in June 2000, following a successful 30 + year career with Ford Motor Company. He offers a wide range of tailored consulting, communications and organizational development services with a special focus on meeting, presentation & event design. His 1st book, *We've Got To Stop Meeting Like This!* (co-authored with Tony Jeary), was published in late 2000, and a handbook, *Meeting Magic!* was published by The WALK THE TALK® Company in late 2001. He and his wife, Marj, live in Northville, Michigan.

Sara Bowling

Sara Bowling, also known as Tony's "Desktop Diva", travels around the globe with Tony to facilitate his sessions from start to finish. She also writes most of his marketing content. Sara holds a graduate degree in English Literature, has ghostwritten several widely un-read books, and receives far too many emails. She resides in the Dallas area with her son, dog and laptop.

Acknowledgements

To George Lowe, my partner on many projects, I appreciate your commitment to excellence in all you do.

Special thanks also to Marc Harty, our internet marketing specialist, whose insight has helped us increase our own email efficiency.

Thanks to the ATW editing team – another great job!

And lastly, this work would not have been possible without the dedication and input of Sara Bowling. Thank you for your tremendous contribution and vision.

Other CornerStone Leadership Books:

Monday Morning Leadership is David Cottrell's newest and best-selling book. It offers unique encouragement and direction that will help you become a better manager, employee, and person. **$12.95**

Listen Up, Leader! Ever wonder what employees think about their leaders? This book tells you the seven characteristics of leadership that people will follow. **$9.95**

Walk the Talk...And Get the Results You Want is a compelling allegory showing how to bring new life to your organization and turn values and ethics into value-added results. **$21.95**

The Manager's Coaching Handbook is a practical guide to improve performance from your superstars, middle stars and falling stars. **$9.95**

Sticking To It: The Art of Adherence reveals the secret to success for high achieving organizations and provides practical advice on how you can win the game of business. **$9.95**

Ethics 4 Everyone provides practical information to guide individual actions, decisions, and daily behaviors. **$9.95**

175 Ways to Get More Done in Less Time has 175 really, really good suggestions that will help you get things done faster...usually better. **$9.95**

180 Ways to Walk the Recognition Talk is packed with proven techniques and practical strategies that will help you encourage positive, productive performance. **$9.95**

136 Effective Presentation Tips is a powerful handbook providing 136 practical, easy to use tips to make every presentation a success. **$9.95**

Becoming the Obvious Choice is a roadmap showing each employee how they can maintain their motivation, develop their hidden talents, and become the best. **$9.95**

Visit www.**cornerstoneleadership**.com
for additional books and resources.

☑ YES! Please send me extra copies of *Too Many Emails!*
1-100 copies $9.95   101-499 copies $8.95   500+ copies $7.95

Too Many Emails   _____ copies X_____   = $_____

Additional Leadership Development Books

Monday Morning Leadership   _____ copies X $12.95   = $_____

Listen Up, Leader!   _____ copies X $9.95   = $_____

Walk the Talk...And Get The Results You Want _____ copies X $21.95 = $_____

The Manager's Coaching Handbook   _____ copies X $9.95   = $_____

Sticking to It: The Art of Adherence   _____ copies X $9.95   = $_____

Ethics 4 Everyone   _____ copies X $9.95   = $_____

175 Ways to Get More Done in Less Time _____ copies X $9.95   = $_____

180 Ways to Walk the Recognition Talk   _____ copies X $9.95   = $_____

136 Effective Presentation Tips   _____ copies X $9.95   = $_____

Becoming the Obvious Choice   _____ copies X $9.95   = $_____

Leadership Development Package   _____ packs X $99.95   = $_____
   (one of each of the 10 books above)

                                   Shipping & Handling $_____

                                   Subtotal $_____

                                   Sales Tax (8.25%-TX Only) $_____

                                   Total (U.S. Dollars Only) $_____

Shipping and Handling Charges

Total $ Amount	Up to $50	$51-$99	$100-$249	$250-$1199	$1200-$3000	$3000+
Charge	$5	$8	$16	$30	$80	$125

Name _____ Job Title _____

Organization _____ Phone _____

Shipping Address _____ Fax _____

Billing Address _____ Email _____

City _____ State _____ Zip _____

❏ Please invoice (Orders over $200) Purchase Order Number (if applicable)_____

Charge Your Order: ❏ MasterCard   ❏ Visa   ❏ American Express

Credit Card Number_____ Exp. Date _____

Signature_____

❏ Check Enclosed (Payable to CornerStone Leadership)

Fax	**Mail**	**Phone**
972.274.2884	P.O. Box 764087	888.789.5323
	Dallas, TX 75376	

www.**cornerstoneleadership**.com

CornerStone
Leadership Institute